THE NATURE KIDS GUIDE TO

BIGHORN SHEEP

DAVID ANDERSON

For information address LP Media Inc. Publishing,
30012 Variolite St NW, Princeton MN 55371
www.lpmedia.org

Publication Data

Bighorn Sheep
The Nature Kid's Guide to Bighorn Sheep — First edition.

Summary: "Learn all about Bighorn Sheep, the Nature Kid Way"
— Provided by publisher.

ISBN: 979-8-89818-149-9

[1. Bighorn Sheep - Non-Fiction] I. Title.

Title: The Nature Kid's Guide to Bighorn Sheep

CONTENTS

ROCKY HEIGHTS

4

Clack! A bighorn sheep stands on a steep cliff.

Bighorn sheep live in the mountains of North America. They make their homes on rocky cliffs and steep slopes. These high places keep them safe from danger.

The mountains can be very cold. Snow covers the peaks in winter. Bighorn sheep have thick coats to stay warm. These coats have two layers of fur for extra warmth.

Rocky ledges are no problem for these sheep. They rest on narrow cliffs and find food on grassy slopes below. Mountains are the perfect home for bighorn sheep.

MOUNTAIN HOMES

Stomp! A bighorn sheep climbs a rocky ridge. It surveys the land below.

Bighorn sheep live across western North America. They roam from Canada down to Mexico.

Different herds live in different places. Some live in the Rocky Mountains. Others live in desert mountains of the Southwest.

Most bighorn sheep move with the seasons. In summer, they climb higher. In winter, they move to lower slopes to find food.

Herds use the same mountain paths year after year. Some trails are hundreds of years old!

SIZE UP

Thump! A ram lands on a ledge. Its big body fits perfectly.

Bighorn sheep have stocky bodies built for climbing. Their legs are short but powerful.

Male sheep are called rams. A ram can weigh more than 300 pounds. Females are called Ewes. They are smaller, weighing about 150 pounds.

The ram's curved horns are hard to miss. They can grow over 3 feet long and curl back around toward his face. Ewes have horns too, but theirs are short and straight.

A ram's horns alone can weigh up to 30 pounds!

CURLY CROWNS

Crack! A ram shakes its huge horns. The curls twist back.

Bighorn sheep are named for their large, curved horns. Rams use their horns to fight other males and show off to females.

The horns curve backward and then forward, making a big spiral shape. These horns never stop growing throughout a ram's life. You can tell a ram's age by counting the rings on its horns.

Horns are made of **keratin**, the same material in your fingernails!

A ram's horns can grow over 3 feet long. That is longer than a baseball bat!

SUPER SENSES

Snort! A ewe lifts her head. Her eyes scan the rocky slope.

Bighorn sheep have amazing eyesight. Their large eyes spot movement from up to a mile away. This helps them see predators early.

Their eyes sit on the sides of their head. This gives them a wide view without turning around.

Bighorn sheep also see well in dim light. Their sharp vision keeps them safe.

A bighorn sheep can spot a moving predator from over a mile away on a clear day.

BUILT TOUGH

Crunch! A ram bumps its head on a rock. It walks away just fine.

Bighorn sheep have very thick skulls. Their skulls are double-layered with spongy bone inside. This special bone absorbs hard hits like a helmet.

This protection matters because rams crash into each other at speeds up to 40 miles per hour. That is as fast as a car on a city street!

Rams fight to show who is strongest. They butt heads to impress the ewes. Their thick skulls let them battle safely.

After head-butting, rams sometimes wobble before walking straight again.

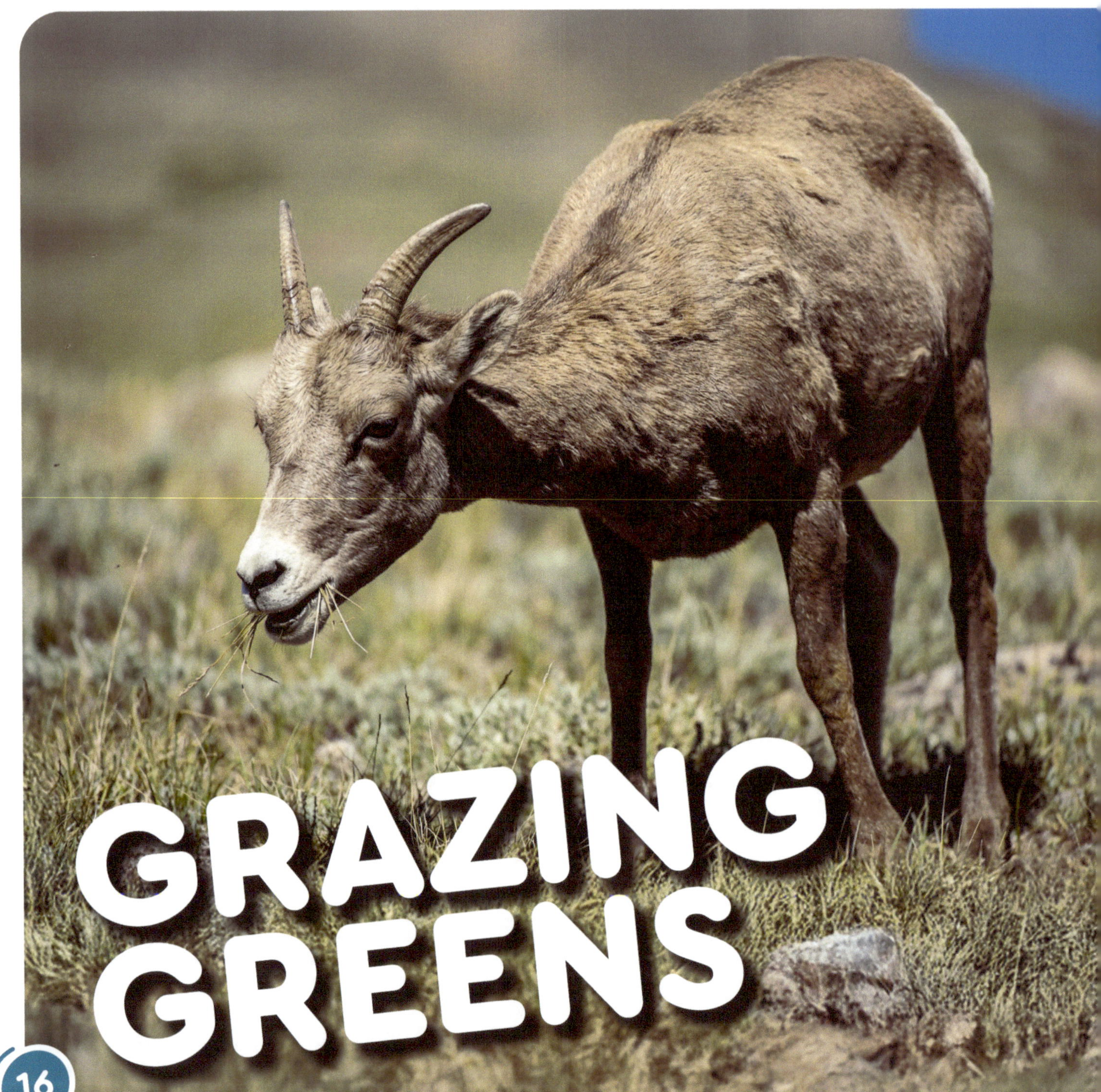

16

Chomp! A ewe bites off some grass. She chews slowly.

Bighorn are **herbivores**. That means the only eat plants. Grasses make up most of their diet in summer.

In winter, food is harder to find. Bighorn sheep eat shrubs, woody plants, and even cacti. They can dig through snow to reach buried plants.

Bighorn sheep do not need much water. They get moisture from the plants they eat. They can go several days without drinking.

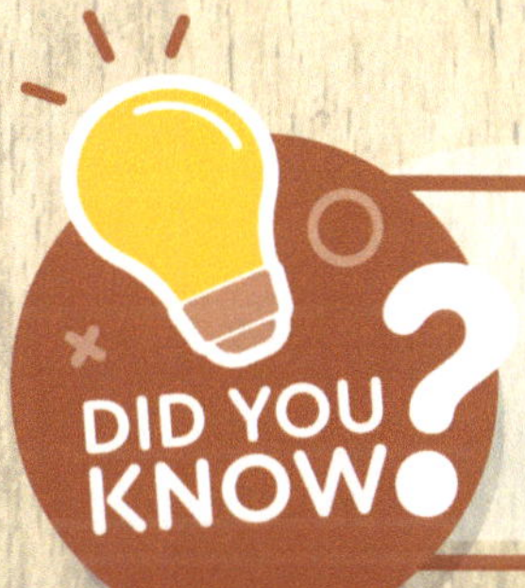

Bighorn sheep spend up to 7 hours eating each day!

SNORTS AND STOMPS

A bighorn's foot stomp sends vibrations through rock that other sheep can feel.

Grunt! A ram stamps its front hoof. Other sheep look up.

Bighorn sheep talk to each other in many ways. They use sounds and body movements to share messages.

Rams make low grunts and snorts. Ewes bleat to call their lambs. Lambs answer with high-pitched calls. Each mother knows her own baby's voice.

Bighorn sheep also use their bodies to communicate. When danger is near, a sheep may make a loud coughing sound as a warning. Rams lower their heads and show off their large horns. These signals help the herd stay safe and connected.

WATCH OUT

Screech! A golden eagle dives from the sky. A lamb runs to its mother.

Bighorn sheep face **predators** like mountain lions, wolves, and eagles. Golden eagles hunt lambs from above. Mountain lions stalk sheep on rocky slopes.

Coyotes, bobcats, and wolves also hunt bighorn sheep. These predators look for young, old, or sick animals that are easier to catch.

Bighorn sheep stay alert to survive. They watch for danger from all directions. Living in groups helps them spot predators faster.

Mountain lions are the main predator of adult bighorn sheep in most areas.

CLIFF ESCAPE

Whoosh! A ewe leaps across a gap and lands safely on the other side.

Bighorn sheep escape danger by running to cliffs. Their hooves grip steep rocks, so most predators cannot follow.

When a sheep spots a threat, it moves fast. It can climb rocky walls that look impossible. The rough hoof pads work like sticky rubber.

Cliffs are the safest place for bighorn sheep. They sleep on narrow ledges at night.

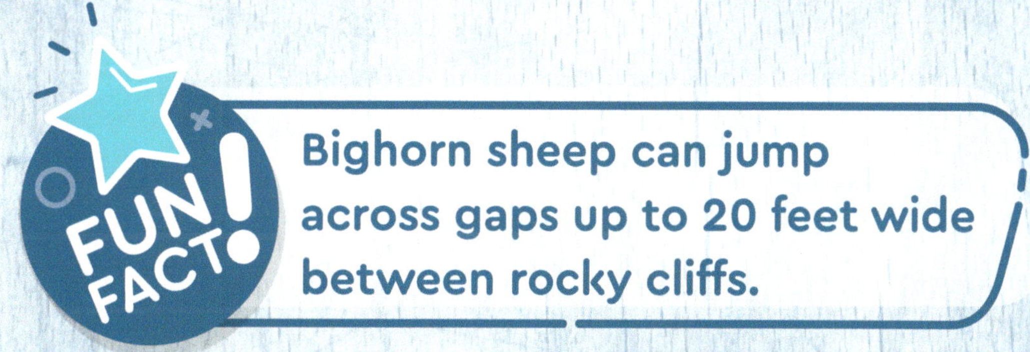

LEAP AND LAND

Click! A ram jumps from a rocky cliff. It bounds down the slope.

Bighorn sheep are amazing jumpers. They can leap across wide gaps and land softly on narrow ledges.

Their strong back legs push them into the air. They jump from rock to rock with ease.

These sheep land safely even when moving fast. They can reach speeds up to 30 miles per hour while running down steep slopes.

Bighorn sheep can land on ledges only 2 inches wide— about as narrow as your thumb!

DAY BY DAY

Stretch! A ewe wakes on a ledge. The sun is rising.

Bighorn sheep start their day at dawn. They climb down from sleeping ledges to find food. Mornings are busy times for grazing.

They eat for several hours. Then they rest and chew their **cud**. This helps them digest tough plants.

Afternoons bring more grazing. As the sun sets, sheep climb back up to safe ledges. They sleep in short bursts through the night.

Bighorn sheep take hundreds of tiny naps each night, rarely sleeping more than 5 minutes at a time.

HERD HANGOUT

Baa! A group of ewes graze together on a grassy slope.

Bighorn sheep live in groups called **herds**. Ewes and lambs stay together all year, while rams form their own groups.

Herds can have 10 to 100 sheep. All those eyes help spot predators and keep everyone safe.

Older ewes lead the herd. They know the best paths to food and water.

Rams only join the ewe herds during mating season in late fall and early winter.

BASHING BATTLES

Thud! Two rams charge at each other. Their horns crash loud.

Male bighorn sheep fight to show strength. They back up and run at each other. Their horns smash together with a loud crack.

These battles can last for hours. Rams hit heads at speeds up to 40 miles per hour. The sound can be heard up to one mile away.

Rams with the biggest horns usually win these fights. The winner gets to mate with the females in the herd.

A ram's skull has two layers of bone. This helps protect its brain during head-bashing battles.

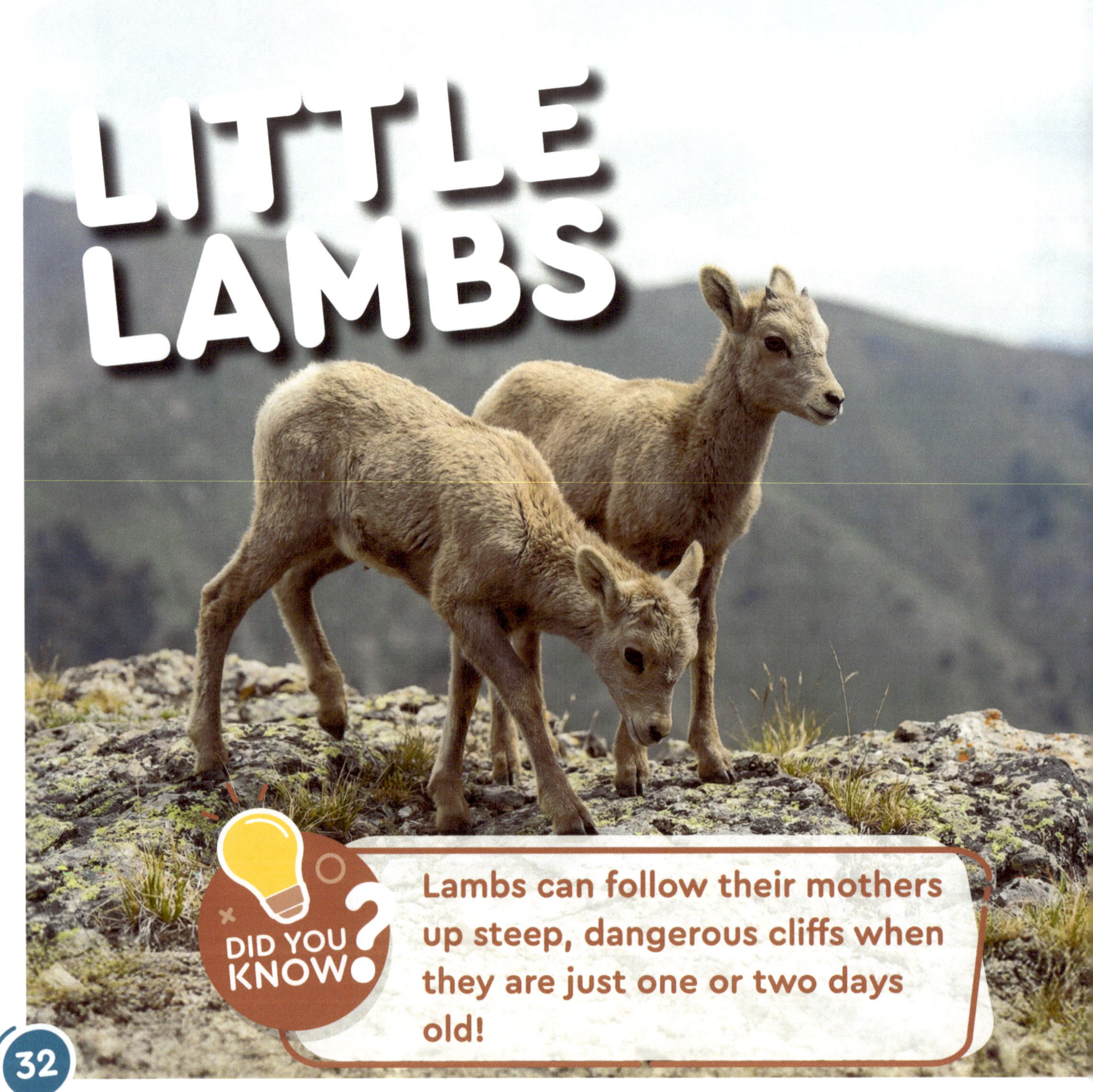

LITTLE LAMBS
DID YOU KNOW?
Lambs can follow their mothers up steep, dangerous cliffs when they are just one or two days old!

Squeak! Two young lambs stand at the top of a ledge.

Baby bighorn sheep are called lambs. They are born in spring on high, rocky ledges. Newborns weigh about 8 to 10 pounds.

Lambs can stand within minutes of being born. They start walking on rocky ground right away. This helps them escape danger fast.

Young lambs drink their mother's milk. After a few weeks, they start nibbling plants too. Lambs stay with their mothers for about a year.

When lambs aren't eating, they love to play! They jump on rocks and chase each other.

TRUST MOM

DID YOU KNOW?
A mother can find her lamb by its voice, even in a crowd of hundreds.

Push! A ewe nudges her lamb away from a steep edge.

Lambs learn where to find food and water by following their mothers. They also follow them to cliffs but learn to climb on their own.

Mothers protect their young from danger. If a predator comes near, the herd groups together to protect the lambs. A mother may stomp or charge to scare it away.

Lambs learn by watching their mothers. They copy how she climbs and where she steps. This helps them survive in the mountains.

PEAK POWERS

Jump! A ram leaps between two cliffs. It lands without slipping.

Bighorn sheep have amazing feet built just for mountain life. Their hooves grip rocks like rubber shoes.

Each hoof is split into two toes that can spread apart to grab the rocks. The outer edges are hard and sharp. The inner pads are soft and grip like rubber. This lets them balance on tiny ledges and leap across gaps in the cliffs.

Bighorn sheep can climb 900 feet of steep slope in just minutes. Their rubbery hoof pads grip rock better than hiking boots.

SAVING SHEEP

A herd of rams walks up a ridge. Their numbers are growing.

Long ago, millions of bighorn sheep roamed North America. Hunting and sickness made their numbers drop to fewer than 25,000.

People worked hard to save them. They passed laws to limit hunting. Rangers also moved healthy sheep to new mountains.

Today, there are over 70,000 bighorn sheep. Scientists still watch over them to keep herds healthy and safe.

FUN FACT!

Conservation groups have programs where people can adopt a bighorn sheep to help protect it.

GLOSSARY

herbivores
Animals that only eat plants.

keratin
The hard material that makes up horns and your fingernails.

predators
Animals that hunt and eat other animals.

cud
Food that comes back up from the stomach to be chewed again.

herds
Groups of animals that live and travel together.